Competitive Swimming

(overleaf)   Martyn Woodroffe, butterfly silver medallist in the 1968 Mexico Olympics, in action

Competitive Swimming

Athole Still

ST MARTIN'S PRESS NEW YORK

This book is dedicated to Andrew K. Robb,
formerly teacher of swimming at Robert Gordon's College,
Aberdeen, who introduced me to this wonderful sport and
who was instrumental in bringing British and Olympic
representation to myself and many other swimmers

Printed in Great Britain

Library of Congress Catalog Card Number: 71-165557
First published in the United States of America in 1971
Reprinted 1973

AFFILIATED PUBLISHERS: Macmillan & Company, Limited, London
Also at Bombay, Calcultta, Madras and Melbourne—The Macmillan
Company of Canada, Limited, Toronto

Contents

	Illustrations	6
	Acknowledgment	8
	Introduction	9
1	The Front Crawl	13
2	The Breast Stroke	36
3	The Butterfly Stroke	48
4	The Backstroke	61
5	Training for Competition	71
6	Reaching a Peak	82
7	Race Day	86
8	Food	93
9	Starts and Turns	97
10	Diving	122
	Conclusion	128

Illustrations

| | Martyn Woodroffe in action | *frontispiece* |
| 1 | Don Schollander | 9 |

FRONT CRAWL

2	Arms-only training	15
3–4	'Head-up' exercise	17
5	Arm recovery	18
6	Correct arm position before entry	19
7	Ideal entry position	20
8	Arm and hand position after entry	21
9	Position at start of push-back	22
10–11	Leg-kick practice	24–25
	The Front Crawl Kick	26–27
12	Legs-only training	28
13–14	Two different breathing positions	32

BREAST STROKE

15–16	Arm pull	37–38
17–18	Recovery	39–40
19	Completion of stroke	41
20–21	Varying leg kicks	42–43
	The Timing of the Breast Stroke	44–45

BUTTERFLY STROKE

22–23	Arm and hand position after entry	49
24	Correct arm position for press	50
25–26	Recovery	51

27	Arm and hand position before entry	52
28	Alan Widdowson in action	52
	The Dolphin Kick and its Timing	54–55
29–32	Dolphin kicking practice	56–57

BACKSTROKE

33	Correct arm position at entry	62
34–37	Arm action during pull	63–66
	The Backstroke Kick (Single Arm Pull)	68–69
38	Martyn Woodroffe with his silver medal	89

THE START

39	Position of feet on starting block	99
40–44	The Dive	100–102
45	Start of 100 metres in Six Nations match	103
46–47	Breast-stroke action after dive	105
48–53	Backstroke start .	107–109

THE TURN

54–55	Breast-stroke and butterfly turn	110–111
56–58	Backstroke turn	114–116
59–61	Front crawl 'tumble' turn	118–121

Acknowledgment

I would like to thank Bert Kinnear, formerly Senior National Technical Officer of the Amateur Swimming Association, for proof-reading my script, and also John Hogg, the Southern Counties National Technical Officer, and some of his swimmers, for kindly agreeing to be photographed during a training session.

A.S.

The frontispiece and Plates 13, 14, 28, 38, 45, 52 and 53 appear by kind permission of Tony Duffy, All-Sport Foto Agency; Plate 1 by kind permission of Wide World Photos; all the other photographs are by Ian Vaughan. The line drawings on pages 26, 27, 44–45, 54–55 and 68–69 are reproduced from the Flicker stop books on swimming, by Athole Still, published by Wolfe Publishing Ltd.

Introduction

'And it's Don Schollander, well ahead now, coming home for another great American victory!' You have probably heard these words, or similar ones, many times as you sit at home watching an international swimming match on television. If the winner was not Don Schollander, one of the world's finest sprinters, it might just as well have been

Don Schollander, breaking the world's 200-meter free-style record at the age of 17. (Wide World)

Mike Burton, Debbie Meyer, or another of America's Olympic champions. But when, with the action over, the picture disappears and you find yourself watching the little white light on the dark screen, do you sometimes dream that *you* had just won a medal for the United States, and that the commentator had been saying *your* name to millions of viewers?

Achieving the things we dream about is never easy, but it is a fact that the more difficult the target, the greater is the sense of satisfaction when it is finally reached. In this book I have tried to put down as simply and clearly as possible the basic rules, which, if followed carefully, might lead you to the highest target of a 'cap' for your country and trips all over the world to National and International meets, and the Olympic Games.

If you are beginning your competitive career, this book will, I hope, help you to understand what your coach is asking you to do in the water or in the gymnasium.

Perhaps, however, you do not have any great aspirations in the competitive field, but merely want to be more proficient as an all-round swimmer. Or you may even be a parent who wants to know more about your child's favourite sport, in order to be able to assist his development. My aim has been to help you also, because this is essentially a book for the interested layman as well as the beginning competitor.

For the active reader, hard work will play a prominent part from now on. But hard work itself, although always of very great value, can lose a great deal of its benefit if it is wrongly applied. If your stroke is a bad one, much of the energy you put into it will be wasted. How often have you seen one swimmer 'attacking' the water, using lots of energy, but being overtaken and passed by another swimmer who is moving steadily through the water with a seemingly effortless stroke? As you read on through this book I hope that you will increase your understanding of the four swimming strokes, and as you understand their techniques you should certainly learn to perform them more effectively.

If you read the book carefully and follow the rules, you will find that you have replaced your 'wish bone' with a solid backbone, which should lead you to success.

1   The Front Crawl

It is generally accepted that the front crawl had its competitive beginnings nearly 100 years ago, in 1873, when an Englishman, John Trudgen, won a race in London by bringing both arms alternately over the water. Up till then the most popular competitive stroke had been the side stroke, originally in the 1840s' with both arms working alternately under water, and then from the 1850s with one arm being recovered over the water and one under the water. Trudgen's leg kick was completely different from the modern front crawl, as he used an ordinary breast-stroke action. But other swimmers were soon copying his arm movements, particularly for short races, as the stroke was very exhausting, and eventually, by the 1890s, the breast-stroke leg action had changed to the scissor-like movement of the side stroke.

The next improvement in the stroke came in 1898, when Arthur Cavill, one of six Australian brothers who were all good competitive swimmers, surprised a London audience by beating a well-known champion using a double over-arm technique, but *with his legs tied*. This seemed to indicate—and correctly so—that the then-popular scissor movement of the legs was actually holding swimmers back. Dick Cavill later added a vertical kicking action of the legs, and by the turn of the century a technique was born which must have looked very like the modern front crawl.

Thereafter the front crawl went through several stages, each with its own particular variation. The early Australian crawl, with a two-beat leg kick, gave way to the American crawl, with its six-beat leg kick. This was the stroke with which Johnny Weismuller, the most famous screen Tarzan, dominated world swimming in the 1920s. Then the Japanese further modified the stroke by being the first to allow the shoulders to roll as the arms entered the water. Generally speaking, they kept the six-beat kick; but because of their smaller stature, they shortened the length of arm on entry to allow themselves more power on the pull.

At the time of writing all the above techniques are being used in top-class competitive swimming, and world records have been set by all of them in recent years. An obvious dilemma therefore faces those who coach or write about swimming—which particular method should be recommended? I myself used a modification of the American six-beat crawl, and as that technique is still used with great success at all levels, my attachment to it is based on more than mere sentiment. But developments in recent years have shown that, for longer races in particular, a four-beat or even two-beat kick can be more efficient, and I will be saying a great deal about these later on.

Body position
Whichever version of the crawl is used, all coaches and students of swimming agree that the body position should be flat and parallel with the surface of the water. The position of the head can vary considerably—from a very high one, with the water surface at about eyebrow level and the face looking directly to the front, to a very low

2 Sally Davison (Chelsea S.C.) demonstrates one of the most indispensable methods of training for the front crawler: the small float is placed between the legs, and only the arms are used for propulsion. For advanced swimmers, no float is used, and the legs are usually held together at the ankles by a circular piece of rubber cut from the inner tube of a used car wheel

one, with all except the crown of the head submerged, and the face therefore looking at the bottom of the pool. As a general rule, sprinters carry their heads higher than middle- and long-distance swimmers. The position of the head will, of course, affect the position of the hips and legs, so that a high head usually means lower hips and legs, and a low head correspondingly higher hips and feet.

The position of the shoulders in relation to the water surface throughout the stroke cycle depends almost entirely on the type of arm action being used. Sprinters usually have the least body roll, and a glance at the strokes of the Olympic 100-metres sprint winners since Weismuller won the title in 1924 amply supports this view. In fact, only Miyazaki (Japan), the winner in 1932, showed any pronounced body roll, although his arm recovery was similar to Weismuller's, and in any case the tremendous success of the Japanese in those Games was due as much as anything to their extremely severe (for those days) training. Now you are no doubt asking yourself which of the body positions will be best for you. I shall be returning to that subject during my general comments at the end of this chapter, but I do not want to recommend a particular position till we have considered the arm and leg action, both of which influence and are influenced by the overall body attitude.

Arm action

The arms are by far the most important propulsive part of the entire stroke. In many swimmers, in fact, the legs may give *no propulsion whatsoever*, even though they are kicking. At first sight this may seem a puzzling thing to say, when everyone knows that it is possible to move quite quickly using legs alone with a float in your hands. We will examine the reasons for this statement very fully in the section on leg action, but I make the point now because I want to stress that *arms* are the thing in modern front-crawl swimming.

To put it at its most simple, the arm action has two main phases: the part out of the water; and the part in the water. Obviously the second phase is by far the more important, because it is then that the forward power is being produced. But the out-of-the-water phase—or 'recovery', as it is usually called—is not totally unimportant. What can be said about the recovery *(3–6)*, however, is that a very wide selection of methods can be used, which are all perfectly acceptable and would not

3 I call this the 'head-up' exercise. It is an excellent method of correcting any misplacing of the hand on entry; the aim is to keep the face entirely clear of the water and watch that arm and hand have the correct attitude on entry. In addition, it forces the swimmer to press down immediately and efficiently with the hand, if he is to keep the head high

4 A continuation of the exercise in Plate 3, showing the ideal hand and arm position, and the visual control that the swimmer has over them

5 *The perfect arm recovery: the arm is well clear of the water, and the elbow is bent to allow a relaxed carry-forward of the forearm and hand. Note also the fairly high head position, which will bring the mouth clear of the surface with a turning, not a lift of the head*

affect your forward speed through the water. The most common recoveries are:

1. A completely straight arm taken over vertically.
2. The peaked elbow with a slightly swinging action.
3. The straight arm taken round parallel to and just above the surface of the water.

I personally much prefer the second type, but I have seen the other two methods used very successfully at the highest level of competition.

What, then, should be avoided in the recovery? In short, any action which upsets the balance of the whole stroke. For example, if you have decided on a particular body position, leg kick, etc., and it is working well in medium-pace practice, but seems to fall apart when you start to sprint, this may well be caused by the recovery.

6 *The correct arm position just before entry: the elbow is higher than the hand, and the entry will obviously be made in line with the shoulder. It is also possible to distinguish under water the considerable bend in the right arm as it pushes back under the body*

As the arms speed up and work more vigorously for sprinting, they may set up a reaction which causes the body to twist or bounce, and this should be avoided.

The 'working' part of the cycle begins at the moment the hand touches the water in front of the head. The acceptable area of entry is between a line drawn straight forward from the nose and another line drawn straight forward from the outside edge of the shoulder. An entry over the centre line would be likely to cause an excessive amount of rolling, and one outside the shoulder line would mean a wastage of time before the hand started working the water in the 'power zone'—this is the area between the two shoulder lines, where any propulsive action will produce the most effect. Think of it like this: if you were lying on the floor in the front-crawl position with your arms both out in front, and you wanted to pull

7　*The ideal entry position for front crawl. Note that the elbow is higher than the hand, which is only slightly cupped*

yourself forward along one of three ropes placed a. outside the left shoulder, b. down the centre line of your body, c. outside the right shoulder, which one would you use? Obviously the centre one, because it is within the 'power zone' in which you can bring your muscles to bear in a *concentrated* area without stretching to the outside.

The hand should enter the water nearly flat, with the elbow slightly bent *(7)*. You may have read or been told that the hand should be 'cupped' in order to 'catch' the water, but if, as an inexperienced swimmer, you think of 'cupping' your hand, you will almost certainly 'cup' it far too much. In fact, if you hold your hand absolutely

8 *The arm and hand position immediately after entry: the elbow is still bent, and the hand is in line with, or just inside, the shoulder*

flat with the thumb in and then depress all your fingers about half an inch, you will have the near-perfect position. The hand is your paddle and it is the overall area that matters, not the depth of the 'cup'.

As you enter the hand, I have found that it is better to dip it very slightly to the outside so that the little finger touches the water first. This helps to avoid one of the

9 The 'press' has been completed, and the hand is in the ideal position, well inside the 'power zone' to begin the push-back. Note that the elbow is still bent, as it should be throughout the entire action from entry till just before the recovery

commonest faults in the arm action, namely to allow the hand to drift outside the imaginary line drawn outside the shoulder. Or, to put it another way, with the little finger just entering first, your automatic tendency should be to pull inwards towards the body; this is good, for you are keeping in the 'power zone'.

At this point in the stroke we can do one of three things:

1. Press straight down and push back. Both with
2. Press down to the centre line and push slightly
   out again to the thigh. bent arms.

3. Press down about a foot, bend the elbow until it almost makes a right angle with the upper arm, and push back with the fingers actually pointing across the body before they finally point down again before recovery.

As with the recovery, all three of these methods have been and are still being used at the highest level of competition, although the evidence suggests that a technique between 1. and 2. is the most efficient—I certainly recommend either of these two to anyone beginning to learn the front crawl *(8, 9)*.

Leg action

Now, to come back to my earlier comment that within the full stroke the leg action often gives no propulsion at all. If you swim 25 yards flat out first with your legs tied, then again holding a small float in your hands and kicking your legs, a comparison of the times will make it quite clear that the arms are a very much more efficient propulsive force. Most swimmers will take 50 per cent longer on legs alone than arms alone. But using *full stroke* with two, four, or six leg kicks to each two arm pulls will always be at least a little faster than the arms-alone time. It would therefore appear that the legs are giving that extra bit of propulsion. This is a wrong conclusion. The correct conclusion is that the legs are *causing* the extra speed, but not through giving additional power. They assist by balancing the stroke and thereby helping to keep the whole body in a position where the much greater propulsive efficiency of the arms can best be used.

If you are still not convinced, just think of a speedboat going through the water at 30 m.p.h. Now imagine that

23

10   Leg-kick practice for beginners can best be done with one hand on the channel and the other flat on the wall with the fingers pointing downwards. Note the very flat body position

you are hanging on to the end of it kicking like fury. Will it go at 30 and a bit m.p.h.? Of course, it won't. In fact, it will only go at 29 and a bit m.p.h., because your body on the end of it will actually slow it down, due to your body's best speed at maximum efficiency being far slower than the boat's.

I have laid particular emphasis on the above points because they explain the most important developments in present-day front-crawl swimming. Looking back over my own career and those of many of my contemporaries in the pre-1960 era, I now realise that by far the most common technical mistake was 'over-kicking'— that is, maintaining a very vigorous leg thrash in the misguided belief that it was increasing the overall speed. The most damaging factor of all, of course, was the complete waste of *energy*, the driving force of the body. Energy is

11 This shows how the legs must be kept close together. Notice also that the right foot at its highest point is barely clear of the surface

closely related to the intake of oxygen, and all our muscles need oxygen to function properly, the amount required being roughly in proportion to the size of the muscle. Just compare the large thigh muscles with the shoulder muscles, and you can easily see the inefficiency of allowing the huge leg muscles to swallow up most of the oxygen intake when, as we have proved, they are giving virtually none of the power.

Provided these factors are well remembered, there is

THE FRONT CRAWL KICK

This sequence shows a leg-kicking exercise which is also an aid to breathing.

Notice how straight the legs should be most of the time. Only on the upward movement is there a slight bending at the knee. Notice

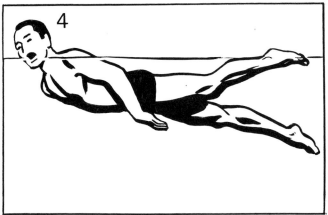

also that it is essentially a thigh movement, clearly shown by the fact that the knees pass each other. When full stroke is swum, the kick would be considerably shallower than shown here, as the emphasis for propulsion would move to the arms. The basic movements, however, would remain the same

12   The most popular method of training on front crawl legs-only. The arms should be straight and the body flat. Front-crawl breathing for beginners can also be practised during this exercise, by putting the face in the water and turning the head in the normal manner for inhalation

certainly no need to give up doing leg-kick practice (*10–12*). In fact, training for legs alone is an excellent part of any programme, particularly early in the season, when it can be a grand way of helping to put the body in good condition.

The action itself is quite simple, although there are certain common faults which it is necessary to guard against. The first thing to remember is that, whether you are doing legs-only practice for power, or swimming full stroke and using the legs for balance and rhythm, the benefit from the legs will come only if they are in the water. This may seem an obvious point to make, but how many crawlers can still be seen, even in a reasonable class of competition, with their feet coming well clear of the water! Avoid this and the cause of it, which is over-bending at the knee. The whole action, whether you are doing two, four, or six beats, is basically a *straight* leg one. Of course, the knees will bend slightly, but this they will do naturally, and it is far better to think of keeping your legs straight than to think of slightly bending the knee. If your mind is on bending the knee, you will almost certainly bend too much, and bring the feet well clear of the water.

The depth of the kick will vary according to whether you are doing full stroke or legs-only. Because they are of very secondary importance in the full stroke, the legs should have a very shallow range, with a maximum depth of about 12 inches. If you think of keeping them within the thickness of the body, you will be about right.

On legs-only, of course, where they are performing a much different function, the maximum depth is often as much as 18 inches. In both cases, it is advisable to have the ankles stretched as much as possible. With full stroke it aids streamlining, and on legs-only the 'whipping' action of a loose ankle on the downward thrash can give good propulsion.

Before we leave the legs, I would like to stress that there is no reason to be wary of learning and practising a six-beat leg action in case you later discover that your natural inclination is towards a two- or four-beat action. Good swimmers know what is going on within their techniques, and you should be able to adapt as you become a more able swimmer. Many of the world's best swimmers have changed their strokes throughout their careers and some have even varied their action between two-, four-, and six-beat, depending on how far they were racing. Roy Saari, of the United States, swam to a world record over

1500 metres using a two-beat action, and sometimes at the beginning and end of this race he would use a six-beat action! He also used six beats over short distances, where he became one of the world's leading sprinters.

Breathing

This is the only swimming fundamental which we are all doing all the time, and yet for some people it is the most difficult part of the crawl stroke. In fact, it is probably more difficult to learn to breathe on the front crawl than on any other stroke, but like anything else good practice can make it easy.

Basically, good breathing for swimmers involves two questions: how? and when?

No matter what type of crawl you are using, a turn of the head will be the minimum requirement for placing the mouth in a safe inhaling position. If your stroke is properly balanced, your mouth should then be in a little trough sheltered by your head and shoulder, and inhalation of air without water should be reasonably easy. As I said earlier, sprinters as a rule lie flatter with less body roll than distance swimmers, and for them the body position should alter as little as possible during the breath, so that the breathing movement is merely the sideways turning of the head which I have just described.

Some swimmers, however, have considerable body (shoulder) roll, and for them the breathing position is nearly over the shoulder, with the mouth almost facing the ceiling of the pool. Either method is acceptable, but bear in mind that it is not *necessary* to roll the shoulders *excessively* in order to breathe, and the overriding principle is that the stroke should decide the breathing position and not vice-versa.

Breathe in through the mouth and out through the mouth (and nose also if you wish). Once air has been taken and the face returned to the water, most swimmers hold the breath and do not begin exhaling until they commence the head turn for the next breath. I myself held the breath till immediately before the mouth broke the surface for the next inhalation. In other words I kept the air in my lungs as long as possible. Most swimmers have fully exhaled before the mouth breaks surface, as the inhalation time is already very limited and should be used mainly for that purpose. Some, however, *finish* exhaling immediately after the mouth breaks surface.

The entire breathing action can be practised admirably while doing legs-only with a float *(12)*. This method is much better than the method often used of standing in the shallow end with the face in the water, because with the kicking exercise you do have forward movement, and the same water turbulence, which you encounter when doing the whole stroke. And also, if you are kicking hard, with those big thigh muscles using up all your oxygen, you will really need to breathe properly!

The best point during the arm cycle at which the breath should be taken is when the arm opposite the breathing side has just entered the water and the breathing arm is beginning its recovery *(13)*. This is by far the most common timing of the breath, although once again we find differences in that some first-class swimmers breathe 'late', i.e., under the recovery arm and when the opposite arm is well under the body *(14)*. Normally, a breath is taken at the same point in each arm cycle, but there are two variations which should be explained: bilateral and breath-holding.

Bilateral refers to the method of breathing after every

third arm stroke, i.e., on alternate sides. This method was once very popular, but is now used by only a handful of swimmers in the top class, and although our own great sprinter Bobby McGregor used it, it is not a technique to be copied for that reason.

Breath-holding is much more common, and is used at certain times by many swimmers who are otherwise normal breathers. It consists of holding the breath, usually at the beginning of a race, while several arm pulls are taken, before settling down to normal breathing. The reasons for this are quite simple. The breathing movement, no matter how smoothly it is made, is bound to interfere with the streamlining of the body and therefore slow down its forward movement. It follows that the longer we can do without a breath, the faster we will go, and this is why some swimmers—mainly sprinters—will not breathe for the first 20 metres or even more of their race. The great danger, of course, is of holding your breath too long, so that an 'oxygen debt' builds up in your body. If this happens, you will more than lose any benefits you may have derived from your breath-holding. It is very much a matter for the individual, so it is really impossible to advise how long the breath should be held. I used this technique myself, and most sprinters still do so, but the point always to remember is that normal breathing *must* be resumed *before* any discomfort whatsoever is felt.

The side on which you decide to breathe is of no importance whatsoever—it is purely a matter of personal

13, 14 Keith Bewley (Southampton) and Tony Jarvis (Otter, London) show their different breathing positions. Jarvis (below) breathes far later in the stroke cycle than most other crawlers

preference. However, if you find that your stroke is developing a heavy dip on the non-breathing side, try breathing to the other side. This will very often stabilise the whole stroke and improve efficiency. It will feel awkward to begin with, but every good crawler should be able to breathe on either side, and a change can often bring a dramatic improvement. Martyn Woodroffe, the butterfly silver medallist at the Mexico Olympics, was always a very ungainly and lopsided front crawler, until his coach made him breathe on the other side. He immediately knocked more than a second off his best 100-yards time, and continued to improve as he persevered with his new breathing method, eventually breaking several British records in his first season as a front crawler.

Conclusion

One thing should be clear from all that I have written about the front crawl, and that is that there is no *one correct* technique. But you should by now have a good idea of the commonest faults and of how to avoid them. You should also now be able to realise why it can be a great mistake to copy a certain swimmer, just because he happens to be successful. The aim of every swimmer should be to make sure first of all that his own *natural* technique does not have any major faults, and then to get on with the hard work and prove that his is 'the' way.

To sum up, in teaching a beginner or learning your first front crawl, bear in mind the following main points, which you will see follow a fairly middle course between the various techniques we have discussed:

1. Fairly flat position with the eyes looking forward and downward (about 45°)

2. Slightly bent arm on recovery, with the elbow pointing towards the ceiling
3. Fairly flat hand entry between the 'nose line' and 'shoulder line', with arm still slightly bent.
4. Press down immediately with the hand and feel that you keep a 'hold' on the water till the hand begins its recovery. The amount of bend on the arm at this stage will depend entirely on how you feel the pressure being maintained
5. Breathe to one side only, once every two arm pulls, and try to breathe by turning rather than lifting the head
6. Allow the arms to dominate the whole stroke, and keep your leg kick shallow. Experiment with two-, four-, and six-beat kicks over various racing distances, to see which suits you best but remember that the six-beat is the basic movement. The others are variations of it
7. Try to cultivate an overall rhythm of constant movement.

2 The Breast Stroke

The breast stroke is almost certainly the oldest method of swimming. It is easy to understand why it would have appealed to prospective swimmers in ancient times, because its very stable position, with the head always clear of the water, is the attitude that a non-swimmer most naturally adopts when confronted with the need to move through water. It is certainly the oldest competitive stroke, and indeed was the only one till the end of the nineteenth century, when the front crawl began to emerge.

Since those early days the breast stroke has, of course, undergone changes, but, unlike the front crawl, there is now almost universal agreement as to what is the fastest and most efficient form of the stroke. The main characteristics of the old stroke were:

1. Wide, shallow arm pull
2. Wide, circular leg kick
3. Long glide after the leg kick, with arms stretched to front
4. Breath taken immediately the arm pull began
5. Main propulsion from the legs

The modern stroke is virtually the opposite of the above in all respects, and the stroke I advocate closely follows that used by the American Chester Jastremski, who in 1961 reduced the existing world record for 200 metres

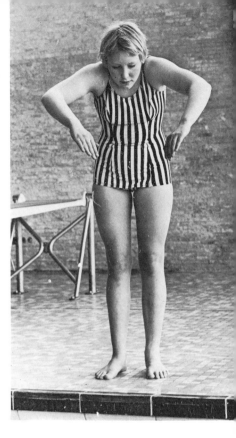

15 Note how the beginning of the modern breast-stroke pull is quite similar to the butterfly and front crawl actions, with the arms bent and the hands pressing down. The head is low, and will remain down till the hands begin to recover

by the huge margin of seven seconds. You will remember from the previous chapter that I do not as a rule advise copying a star performer. I do so now because the Jastremski stroke was 'designed' by Dr James Counselman, swimming coach of Indiana University, because he felt that the old method was not sufficiently streamlined and efficient. The *principles* on which he worked have proved to be mechanically sound, so it is logical to copy

16 *The pull is short, narrow and fast, and here we already see the beginning of the recovery phase, with both hands moving inwards and the head raised for the breath*

them, without slavishly copying the exact stroke of his great pupil, who in spite of his success never won an Olympic title, although he competed in three Games.

Body position
The body should be as flat as possible, and particular care should be taken to try to remain flat when the head is being raised for the breath. If the head movement is a

17   The head has just lifted for the breath as the hands recover in front of the face. The legs are also recovering at this point

rapid and small one, the overall position should not be too adversely affected.

Arm action
The main developments in the arm movement are that it is narrower, deeper, and more vigorous than in the classic breast stroke. If we begin at the point when both arms are extended in front of the face, the first movement will in fact be quite similar to the front crawl, with the palms pressing downwards, but slightly outwards, to balance the body, and the elbows slightly bent *(15, 16)*. The outward motion should not progress more than 12 inches beyond

18 A front view of Plate 17. Note that the hands are very close to the chest and that they are in an almost flat position, in order to offer as little resistance to the water as possible

the width of the shoulders (remember the 'power zone'), and the downward press should end about six inches before the hands approach the vertical plane of the shoulders, when the hands should be brought together very quickly for the forward stretch. At this point in the old stroke, there was always a glide to allow the leg propulsion to have its full effect. Nowadays, however, the glide is definitely *out*, and the next stroke cycle begins immediately the arms are fully extended.

The whole idea of gliding in swimming was, I think, very well summed up by the great American coach Matt Mann. 'When you're gliding, the other fellow may be

19 The hands and arms have stretched forward to form the most streamlined and flat position of the entire breast-stroke cycle. At this point the feet will have just met at the end of the kick

pulling!' He was in fact referring to the front crawl, but it is a principle which should always be borne in mind in modern competitive swimming, where the top performers are fit enough to keep the stroke 'working' all the time.

This narrower, deeper arm pull permits a faster recovery of the hands, and with the resulting increase in stroke tempo, the modern breast stroke joins the other strokes as being dominated by the arms.

This extremely vigorous arm action, by the way, calls for great forearm strength, and it is advisable to work on this during gym and weight-training work in the off season.

20 The more conventional breast-stroke kick, with a wider action than in Plate 21. The legs are at their widest point, while moving backwards till the feet meet

Leg action

In keeping with the arms, the legs also have a narrow, very fast action, and we will begin to examine it at the point when the legs are straight and together after the actual kick.

Remembering that the aim is to keep the body as flat as possible, try not to bring the upper leg too far forward in the leg recovery. The knees should be scarcely apart during this recovery, certainly not outside shoulder width, and the heels drawn up as close as possible to the seat *(21)*. From this point the feet are driven straight back with a slightly circular motion. I hasten to stress,

21 The legs are moving backwards before they snap together at the end of the kick. This action is very close to the Jastremski kick, which is narrower than most other variations. Note how the feet are splayed outwards to present the insides of the ankles backwards to the water

however, that the movement is much more backward than circular.

In this modern stroke the heels from the seat to the end of the kick would describe a narrow melon shape. In the old stroke they would have drawn a lovely circle (*20*).

Breathing

Breast-stroke breathing is exactly the same as for front crawl in respect of its method (i.e., explosive) and also timing (i.e., at the end of the propulsive arm movement). But it was not always so. The timing of the breath has

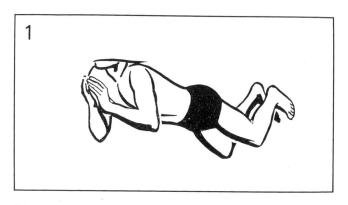

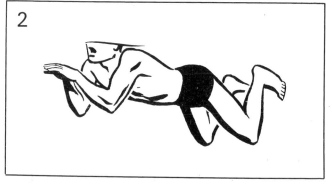

THE TIMING OF THE BREAST STROKE

This sequence gives an impression of the timing of the late-breathing breast stroke used by former world record holder Chester Jastremski (USA):

1. The head has lifted for the breath as the arms complete their recovery, and the legs begin theirs

2. The face drops back into the water as the arms begin to move forward into the stretch. The legs have reached the position of maximum bend, and are starting to move backwards for the kick.

Note the narrowness of the kick, and the wide angle between the trunk of the body and the thighs

3. As the arms continue to reach forward, the feet turn outwards and move almost straight backwards. There is only a slight widening of the kick

4. The body is very flat as the arms complete the stretch. Note how the hands are already turning outwards for the next pull before the feet have met at the end of the kick. This shows the 'continuous motion' character of this technique with the total absence of a glide

altered so much in the new stroke in relation to the old breast stroke, that the new stroke which I have been describing here is often called quite simply the 'late-breathing' breast stroke, and is almost universally used by the leading men and women in the world.

This modern timing springs from the very logical thinking that the body should be kept as streamlined as possible during the propulsive phases. It would now seem to be obvious that the best time to breathe in breast stroke must be when the arms have completed their action, and the legs are about to begin theirs. Yet for many, many years nearly all breast-stroke swimmers breathed as they began their arm pull, and as the legs were considered the main source of power little effort was made to streamline (and lie flat) till the kick came. The head was lifted high, and often the shoulders also, offering great resistance to the water and wasting the arm pull.

Nowadays one must concentrate on lying flat, keeping the head and shoulders in the water till the arms are about to begin their recovery, then the head, and *only* the head lifts and drops again very quickly before the arm stretch and the leg kick.

If you have been using the older-type breast stroke I strongly advise you to change to the late-breathing variety, bearing in mind also, of course, the other points mentioned, particularly the narrowing-down of the whole stroke. I believe Jastremski's coach encouraged him to think of 'swimming through a pipe', and I find this a particularly vivid way of approaching this entire stroke.

Three legal points must be made before we leave the breast stroke: firstly, the shoulders must be parallel with the water at all times; secondly, both legs in the kick must perform absolutely similar movements on the same plane. This last statement simply means that one leg must not be higher or lower than the other, or slightly ahead or behind the other in the cycle. If they are not completely similar, one risks a 'screw kick' which causes disqualification. Thirdly, the body must never be completely submerged, except when starting and turning.

3 The Butterfly Stroke

This stroke was the last of the four swimming methods to be accepted for international competition. It originally developed in the 1930s with the addition of the double overarm action to the already established breast stroke, and was swum in breast-stroke races. As with the early days of the front crawl, most swimmers thought it too strenuous for anything longer than a sprint, but certainly in short races it proved faster than the orthodox breast stroke. After the 1952 Olympics however, the two strokes were separated and the butterfly became a stroke in its own right, as it fully deserved, for with the added development of the double up-and-down, fish-tail movement of the legs, the modern stroke no longer resembled the breast stroke in the slightest. Nowadays it is the second fastest of the four strokes, but undoubtedly the most strenuous.

Body position
As flat as the undulating motion of the 'dolphin' kick will allow.

Arm action
As in the front crawl, the arms are the main source of propulsion, although the legs also give power, much more so than in front crawl.

The arms begin their cycle in the forward position, on

48

22   Gillian Trees (St. James S.C.) demonstrates the correct butterfly arm position just after the hands have entered the water. At this point the hands would already have 'caught' the water and be beginning their downward press

23   A side view of Plate 22, showing how the hands almost form a continuous straight line with the forearms. Beginners must guard against the common fault of cupping the hands too much and therefore reducing the area of 'catch'

either side of the nose, but not outside the shoulder line. This you will see is identical with the single arm entry for front crawl, and the similarity does not end there, for the

49

24 *The correct position for the arms as they press under the body. Note how the elbows are bent, making it much easier to push the hands straight back in the most efficient manner*

hands also have the crawl position and the arms are again slightly bent at the elbow *(22, 23)*.

Normally the hands are pressed straight down to a point fairly central under the body *(24)*, the depth or amount of elbow bend being decided by the strength of the swimmer. One thing is certain, however—a *completely* straight arm is not efficient, and I personally recommend a bend of up to a right angle, before the hands

25　The body at its highest point as the breath is taken. The arms
have just begun their recovery, and the splash indicates that the
second kick of the cycle has just occurred

26　A front view taken only a split second after Plate 25, yet the
face is already dropping back into the water and the arms are just
passing shoulder level. Note that the arms are quite clear of the
water and therefore not retarding the forward movement in any way

27   An excellent shot showing the relaxed arms and hands about to enter the water in the correct position in line with the shoulders

28   Alan Widdowson (Nottingham) shows the butterfly stroke which brought him victory for Britain in a recent international match. Alan's arms show a bend which is not typical of most butterfliers

part and the arms straighten for the final push to just outside the thighs.

During the recovery *(25–28)* there is usually much less of the peaked elbow as seen in the crawl. The arms are straighter and higher, and whereas I like to think of the crawl recovery as a 'carry' forward of the arm, the butterfly recovery is a much speedier 'fling'. The recovery must be very fast, because, unlike the crawl, where one arm is still giving major propulsion, in the butterfly, propulsion has almost ceased, and although there has been a kick as the hands left the water, this will more or less only maintain the body's position rather than drive it forward.

Leg action

After early experiments with one- and three-beat leg kicks, it is now universally accepted that the two-beat is by far the most efficient timing of the legs.

The kick originates in the hip, and consists of a very vigorous downward 'whip' with both legs working absolutely in unison. It is essential to keep the legs and feet on the same plane, because disqualification will result if one foot is even slightly ahead of the other in the kicking action. This would be considered a flutter kick, which is not permissible.

The main points to bear in mind are that the hips should be kept high and that there should not be too much bending at the knees. At the highest point in the action the feet should barely break the surface, and at the deepest point the heels should not be more than 12 inches below the surface. Flexible ankles will greatly assist the 'whip' in the kick, and it is better to turn the feet slightly inwards in a 'pigeon-toed' fashion to help the ankle extension.

THE DOLPHIN KICK AND ITS TIMING

1. The legs are in their position of maximum bend as the arms enter the water

2. The hands immediately begin their press, and at the same time the legs whip straight down and back. Note how the hips lift slightly.

3. The legs approach their bent position again as the arms begin the push backwards

4. The second kick comes as the push of the hands ends and the arms begin to recover

29 A beginner can practise the dolphin kick at the poolside. A downward kick has just been completed, with the legs perfectly straight and the hips at their highest position, near to or just breaking the surface

30 The knees bend and the feet begin to rise in preparation for the next kick. The splash in the centre gives some idea of the vigorous downward movement of the hips at this point

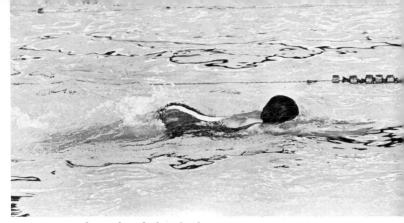

31 A more advanced method of dolphin kicking practice, using a small float. Note how high the hips rise at their highest point

32 A continuation of Plate 31, with the body still stretching forward as the hips drop and the feet rise. Note the shallow 'S' formation from hands to feet

As you will see from that description, the kick is a comparatively shallow one, which allows the body to maintain a fairly flat position throughout the entire cycle. For the beginner, the leg kick can be profitably practised at the poolside, holding the rail or scum channel, with the forearms vertically on the pool wall *(29, 30)*.

The first kick should be timed to coincide with the entry of the hands, and the second with their final push immediately before the recovery. This timing can be practised simply by standing (not in the water), and swinging your arms in the correct butterfly manner. As the arms reach the position directly in front of you, bend your knees slightly and say 'Kick!' Quickly straighten the legs, and, as the arms come to the hips, repeat the process. Eventually you will be able to do this at a fair speed, and you will then have the 'feel' of this timing, which is very important to the correct performance of the stroke.

Breathing
The breath is usually taken once to every arm cycle. Some swimmers when racing take more than one arm stroke to each breath, but this is an advanced practice, to be used only by the most fit and experienced performers. Butterfly swimming is probably the most demanding of all forms of physical exercise, and a frequent supply of oxygen is of very great importance.

Having said that, however, I would like to add that I consider it an excellent exercise to sprint flat out without breathing for distances of up to about 25 metres. The absence of any body lift for breathing will help you keep a very flat, and therefore ideally efficient, position, and you will probably find that you can do your fastest times for short sprints in this manner. Only when breathing is fully mastered should you attempt this method with two or even three arm pulls per breath in sprint races (cf. p. 33).

Most of the top-class butterfliers take the breath late in the arm cycle, where it usually coincides with the second kick and final push of the hands. There are sound reasons for this being the best point. The greatest propulsion in the entire stroke comes between the point of entry of the hands and their arrival directly under the body. It is obviously best, therefore, that the body should be in its most streamlined and flat position in order to take full advantage of the power. A breath anywhere in this section, with the inevitable head and shoulder lift, is clearly inadvisable.

The final question to answer about breathing is whether the head should be turned to the side as in front crawl, or lifted directly to the front. Although in the early years of the stroke's development the head turn was favoured, nowadays the forward lift is by far the more popular. I feel that this has been brought about naturally by the swimmers themselves, not by coaching. Frankly, I found it slightly uncomfortable to turn the head to the side, and I also found it increased the frequency of unwanted mouthfuls of water.

It would certainly seem that the head turn with no lifting, and the body therefore flatter, *should* be the most efficient, but it has been rejected by most butterfliers. The main point to bear in mind about forward breathing, however, is that ideally *only* the head should lift, and although it is impossible not to have some raising of the shoulders with the arms commencing their recovery, nevertheless it should be kept to a minimum.

Butterfly is unquestionably the most exhausting of the

four strokes, but I consider it to be second only to the backstroke in its technical simplicity, although I know that many will not agree with me. Anyway, I recommend that it be practised very early in any swimmer's career.

4 The Backstroke

Backstroke swimming developed directly from the breast stroke, and the earliest version was, in fact, an exact copy of the breast stroke done on the back. But the awkward recovery of the arms over the chest and face was soon superseded by a straight, double overarm action. This stroke became known as the Old English backstroke, and was the stroke used when competitive backstroke races began about 1903. In the beginning, one leg kick was taken to each double arm action, but within a few years the arms were being used alternately, with one leg kick to each single arm pull.

The stroke was now beginning to appear something like the present-day one, and the transformation was completed at Stockholm in 1912, when the American Harry Hebner added a crawl kick to the alternate arm action, and won the Olympic gold medal.

Most of the early back-crawlers had a high arm recovery and a fairly deep pull, but in the mid-thirties, the American Adolph Kiefer set a new fashion, with a very low recovery, very shallow pull, and the arms absolutely straight throughout the action. This technique lasted until David Theile (Australia) won gold medals in the 1956 and 1960 Olympics using the bent arm pull which is now accepted as the most efficient action.

33 The correct arm position at the point of entry. The arm is comfortable beside the head, without the over-extension at the shoulder which results from pushing the hand behind the head. Note how the palm of the hand is inclined towards the surface of the water

Body position

As with the other strokes, a flat position is also best for backstroke. If the head is held well back in the water, it will be easier to lie perfectly flat, as there will be no tendency for the hips to drop. This was a common fault in many backstrokers who favoured the head-up position which was fashionable for many years.

34 As the arm moves round in the first part of the pull, the elbow bend is already noticeable. The palm of the hand is pressing downwards rather than straight backwards to the feet

Arm action

The arms are the most important propulsive agents, and it has now been scientifically proved that the shallow, straight arm pull, which was used almost universally from the 1930s to the 1950s, is not the most efficient arm action. Nowadays the bent arm pull *(33–37)* is clearly here to stay, and this is really the only major development in the stroke since the days of Kiefer.

The hands should enter the water with the arm straight and as close to the head as is possible without causing discomfort, or the side-to-side movement of the body, which can result from over-reaching, if the shoulder

35 As the arm passes the level of the shoulders the bend is at its most pronounced and the hand should still be pressing downwards— even more, in fact, than in this photograph

joint is not particularly flexible. On no account should the hands enter further from the head than 11 o'clock and 1 o'clock, if we imagine the head as the centre of a clock face. The further out the hands are from the ideal position, the less benefit will be derived from the bent arm pull.

Immediately the hand enters the water it should begin to press downward towards the feet, and *at the same time* the arm should progressively bend at the elbow, till the forearm and upper arm make approximately a right angle as they pass the level of the shoulders.

It is virtually impossible to be more specific than this

36   Near the end of the action, the arm is completely straight, but note how the hand has flexed backwards at the wrist to maintain a proper hold of the water

about the amount of elbow bend to use, because it will vary from swimmer to swimmer. Some of the best backstrokers have less than 90 degrees of maximum bend, and some have more. You yourself must decide by 'feel'. You should know when you have a real 'hold' of the water—the pressure will be greatest then—so try to keep the pressure up throughout the movement. By experimenting you will find out what is best for you.

An important point to watch throughout most of this section of the movement is that the elbow as it bends should not be allowed to precede the hand. The hand should be ahead of the elbow, so that you feel you are

65

37 Here is the final position, with the arm perfectly straight and the hand in alignment with the forearm, after completing a vigorous push to a point under *the hip*

pressing or pushing rather than pulling. At the very beginning of the arm action, of course, there will be a very small area of 'pull' as the elbow begins to bend.

As the hand passes the shoulder, the palm will gradually face more towards the bottom of the pool, and the final push, with the arm straightening itself completely, should bring the hand about six inches below hip level. At this point the palm should be turned towards the body, so that the hand will have the least possible water resistance to overcome as it begins the recovery.

Leg action

I believe that the legs should be subordinated to the arms, as they are in front crawl, particularly nowadays with the bent arm pull, which is mechanically much more similar to the front crawl than the Kiefer-type backstroke was. I also believe, however, that the backstroke leg kick does give actual propulsion as well as balance to the stroke, and this seems to be borne out by the fact that most good backstrokers still use an orthodox six-beat kick, as opposed to the wide variety of kicks successfully used by top-line front-crawlers.

The action itself is almost identical with that of kicking a football. As the upper leg drops, the knee bends about 45 degrees to prepare for the very vigorous upward whip, when the real power is applied. At the end of the kick the whole leg is once again completely straight.

The foot should be flexed as much as possible so that the toes point to the receding end of the pool. It will increase your ankle flexion to turn the feet slightly inwards, so that if you are swimming in the middle lane of the pool your right foot should kick roughly towards the left corner and your left foot towards the right corner.

Do not make the common mistake of kicking from the knee only. The power must come from the hip, and you will guarantee this if you concentrate on making the knees pass each other. Neither knee should ever break the surface, but there should be a space of a few inches between the back of the upper knee and the top of the lower knee when the legs are at opposite ends of the action.

The coordination of the legs and arms is one which gives complete balance to the whole stroke. As one arm is beginning the pull, the *opposite* leg is kicking downward. During this same arm pull, the opposite leg will kick

THE BACKSTROKE KICK (SINGLE ARM PULL)

1. Note the completely straight right leg with flexed foot as the kick is delivered at the surface

2. As the right leg drops, the knee bends considerably into a 'football kicking' position

3. Note the space between the knees, showing that there must be whole leg movement from the thigh, before the knee bends
4. The left leg delivers its kick. The final point to note is that the knees never break surface

upward, and as it commences its second downward action the other arm is ready for the next pull.

It is obviously confusing, however, to think of this, if you are a learner, so at the beginning concentrate separately on the arms and legs. The leg kick can be practised at the poolside, either with the arms outstretched along the scum channel or with the hands clasping the wall beside each ear with the elbows pointing directly at the feet. This static position is extremely good for a beginner, because he can see clearly whether his legs are obeying the rules set down earlier.

The next stage is swimming legs-only, with the arms by the side and the hands gently pushing the water towards the feet. And the most advanced exercise, used by all serious competitive swimmers, is with the arms outstretched alongside the head and the hands clasped. When you can perform this respectably well, your kick should be a good one.

The arm action can be practised very easily by holding a float between the knees, and the correct coordination of the two will follow very naturally with practice. But always bear in mind that your arms are the main source of power, so do not over-kick and tire yourself unnecessarily.

5 Training for Competition

The days when hard training was considered to mean a swim of a few hundred yards several times a week during the competitive season have long since disappeared. Nowadays it would be nearly impossible for anybody, unless very gifted naturally, to achieve good county competitive standard on less than $1\frac{1}{2}$ miles daily training on six days of the week. And the great science which modern training has become means that it will really be work, which will hurt. But if you follow the fairly simple rules, then you will know that each little ache, each time you decide to stick to your predecided plan, when you already feel exhausted, will bring you a valuable step nearer the goal you have set yourself.

By its nature, this book cannot cover training for every stroke, every distance and every standard of swimmer. In any case, I do not think it would be a very good idea, because something will always upset your plans and you yourself will have to adjust your training accordingly. I will therefore concentrate on explaining how and why things are done so that you can do your own thinking—for as you progress, it will become increasingly important for you to be able to work on your own and make your own decisions.

The schedules which I quote will be roughly for the good-class county swimmer whose racing distance is 100 yards. A beginning competitor or one with only club ambitions would do less than half the quantities mentioned. But a top-flight international performer would probably do two to three times as much. You will also obviously have to increase the distances if you are a middle-distance or distance swimmer.

On this subject of 'type' (i.e., distance) of swimmer, I would like to stress now that I strongly recommend *all* beginning competitors to do middle- and long-distance work. The time for specialisation on sprinting will come later, when and if you show an aptitude for this. But in any case, any early distance work you do will greatly increase your endurance and stand you in good stead, even if you turn out a pure sprinter.

Before we consider actual schedules, let us look at the year as a whole and decide how we should divide it up.

Arranging the season
In Europe and in the Northern Hemisphere generally, the really important swimming events usually come in the late summer and early autumn. Most swimmers will want to be at their best at this time, so all your training over the previous months should be directed towards this period. Bearing this in mind, the year falls naturally into three sections:

1. Winter period (approximately October–March)

2. Pre-competitive period (April–June)

3. Competitive period (July–September)

Each period has a character of its own, which we will now discuss in detail.

Winter training

For most swimmers this is the most enjoyable time of all because of the great variety of work done, and because also the water work should never be really exhausting.

Basically the following types of exercise should be done at this time:

1. Fairly long swims on full stroke, arms-only and legs-only
2. Regular swims on other strokes and medleys
3. Exercises on stroke technique
4. Starts and turns
5. Gymnasium work
6. Games—football, rugby, basketball, volleyball and hockey
7. Cross-country running, walking and skiing

From the above it is obvious that the main aim at this stage is good all-round body fitness, and the great variety of activities listed above (and there are many others) should guarantee that your mental condition is also excellent. The hardest work will be the gymnasium work, where you should do exercises for mobility and strength and also weight-training.

It is really quite impossible and even unwise to advise on weight-training, because the differences between one individual and the next in relation to setting exercises with weights can be quite enormous. There are, however, many excellent short books on this subject which may be consulted. Do not, however, venture into the field of weight-training without first of all consulting an expert, as one can very easily cause an injury by using excessive weights.

For the first two months or so of this five to six month

stage, I believe the main emphasis should be on the 'other' activities listed above. A typical week might be:

MONDAY 30 minutes gym

TUESDAY 1500 yards mixed swimming

WEDNESDAY Gym

THURSDAY 1500 yards mixed swimming

FRIDAY Gym

SATURDAY Any of 6. and 7. on page 73

Some coaches believe in swimming every day, even during this early stage, and I have nothing against it provided that the swimmer *feels* like swimming every day. But I really do believe it would be wrong to insist on it if the swimmer has had a hard season. Changes are good for one, I think.

After a complete rest over the Christmas and New Year period, the January schedule should have swimming five or six days a week, with one or two gym sessions still fitted in if possible. Ideally, swimming can be done immediately after gym or weight-training, and I always found this an excellent way of helping me to 'feel' the water, with my muscles still aching from the land work.

The water sessions should be similar to those at the beginning of this period, except that the amount should have crept up to 2000 yards plus. Again, keep it as varied as possible, and don't be afraid to throw in a straight 2000-yard swim now and again, even though you may be a sprinter. You should be very surprised to learn how many top-class sprinters were originally middle- and long-distance performers.

A typical week's swimming might look like this:

MONDAY 400 swim, 400 legs, 400 arms, 200 medley, 3 ×
200 yards, 4 × 25 yards

TUESDAY 2000-yard swim

WEDNESDAY 250 swim, 1000 legs, 500 arms, 100 medley,
2 × 100 yards

THURSDAY 1000 swim (fast-, medium-, slow-pace variation
as you feel like it), 500 arms, 250 legs, 4 × 25 legs,
4 × 25 arms (both fast)

FRIDAY 400 medley, 1000 arms, 500 legs, 4 × 100 swim

SATURDAY 500 swim, 500 legs, 500 arms, 25 × 25 sprints,
all strokes arms, legs, etc.

Now you will notice that I am introducing some repetition
swims, e.g., 3 × 200, 4 × 100, etc. This is the beginnings
of what is called Controlled Interval Training (C.I.M.),
and this method will form the basis of almost all your
training later in the year.

Add about one-fifth on to your best time for the
distance, and try to repeat that time with as little rest as
you need between each swim—e.g., if your best time for
100 is 55 seconds, try to do 4 × 66 seconds. At the
beginning, try 60-second rests for 50s and two-minute
rests for 100s. Times of 65, 66, 66, 65 would be very good.
Times of 60, 65, 68, 70 would be bad, as they are missing
one of the main points of the exercise, which is to intro-
duce an idea of pacing.

By the end of these few months of very varied work,
you should be feeling really fresh and ready for the 'big
push' from spring onwards. Now the work begins with a
vengeance, but if you have prepared your stroke and your
body properly throughout the winter, you will have
nothing to fear from the next stage of training.

Pre-competitive training

During this stage our county swimmer will have stepped up his training load to around 3000 yards. He will be doing this in one session daily (except Sunday), but most international-class swimmers will be doing two training stints, usually early morning and late afternoon.

Although the quantity has increased, there should be an even more striking improvement in the quality. All repetitions will be accurately timed, and longer rests will be taken to ensure a faster overall average. I also strongly advise the arms-only and legs-only work to be done in repetitions, with set rest periods and target times.

Now you can see that the clock has suddenly taken an important place in all your training. Do not, however, make the mistake of 'racing the clock'. This is not the object of the exercise, which is gradually to build up the resistance of your body and your stroke to the slowly increasing stress of your own improving target times. You yourself, and your coach, will decide the targets and rest periods, and you must aim to repeat them in a controlled (even though effortful) manner.

Many coaches continue to use weight-training and gym work during this stage, and I am in agreement with this, particularly if the swimmer in question needs more body strength. But even those swimmers who have plenty of strength could still benefit from one land training session per week.

A typical week's training might look like this:

MONDAY 500 warm-up, 2 × 200 legs, 3 × 200 arms, 200 medley, 10 × 100 swim, 200 medley, 4 × 25 sprints

TUESDAY 500 warm-up, 500 legs, 2 × 400 swim, 200 medley, 5 × 200 arms, 4 × 25 sprints

WEDNESDAY 500 warm-up, 400 arms, 6 × 100 legs, 5 × 200 swim, 200 medley, 4 × 50 sprints

THURSDAY 500 warm-up, 16 × 50, 200 medley, 2 × 400 arms, 16 × 25 mixed any way

FRIDAY 500 warm-up, 2000 swim (90 per cent), 200 medley, 4 × 50

SATURDAY 500 warm-up, 2 × 400 legs, 10 × 100 arms, 200 medley, 10 × 50

Notes

1. As the quality and effort of the training is now greatly increased, I consider a *proper* warm-up essential to a good work-out. By 'proper', I mean that it should not be a leisurely stroll up and down the pool, but several hundred yards of effort which should leave you feeling warm and probably sweating slightly.

What you do during the 500 yards I have set aside for warm-up is your own affair. Experiment, and decide what and how much feels best for you, but all-stroke swimming is very popular and extremely beneficial.

2. All the above repetitions should be done with longer rests than in the previous stage of training, with about one-tenth added to your best times for the individual target times. Approximate rest periods would be $1\frac{1}{2}$ minutes for 50s, three minutes for 100s, five minutes for 400s.

Remember the aim is to hit or better the target *every* time. If you are constantly slow or much faster, adjust the targets or rest intervals.

3. Hundred per cent effort time trials, on races with the training group, form an important part of any programme, and although I have not indicated any in my suggested schedules, they should take place, not more

than once a week, but not less than once a fortnight. If the swimmer is keen enough, he himself can decide when to do one, as there are definitely spells when you feel like 'having a go'. Provided that the desire is frequent enough, I think this is as good as the coach insisting on a time trial when the swimmer might prefer not to.

Now I do not wish to be misunderstood on this point. The coach is the boss, but flexibility between master and pupil on decisions like this can only lead to a good relationship and inevitably good performances.

4. If there are any minor competitions during this period, they should be taken in their stride with no special adjustment made to the training. A later section on 'the taper' will explain how to deal with any fairly important event, which comes earlier than the season's main competitive period.

5. All training swims should be noted down in your log book. This is extremely important, because you will be able to look back over them and see in detail whether certain schedules produced the required result or not.

The competitive period

You are now in the high season and your training will be entirely based on Controlled Interval Swimming. Our county sprinter will probably be doing only about 1500 yards a day, most of it on full stroke and mainly divided into repetition 25s, 50s, 75s and 100s, but he will also occasionally do repetitions over 'the distance' of 200s and 400s.

Some swimmers and coaches increase the training load in the competitive season; frankly, there is no hard-and-fast rule about this. I have no objections provided that the swimmer does not become jaded or stale. I consider it of paramount importance that a swimmer arrives fresh and rested for his big event, and if this can be achieved after an increased training load, so much the better. But I now know, from bitter experience, that I seldom arrived in that condition during the middle part of my career, and I often paid the price in mediocre performances. This was not the result of bad coaching—I had an excellent coach—but for some years I had to coach myself, and a mixture of keenness and stupidity made me do *very* heavy training loads (8000–12,000 yards up to 1960). I did this kind of work during the competitive season, without using a 'taper', and suffered accordingly. At the end of my career I cut down the load to about 4000 yards (2000 C.I.M.) and never did a bad swim.

Anyway, I hope I have made my point very clear—you will be competing in very important races regularly throughout this period, so make sure that you *feel* like racing.

All the training done in this period must be high-quality and high-effort. The interval training will continue along the already established lines, but now you must add very high-quality swims (95 per cent), naturally with much longer rests. A swimmer with a best 100 of 55 seconds might do 4×100 in 57/58 seconds with 10 or 15 minutes' rest, or similar 50s with five minutes' rest. If you find that taking long rests is impracticable because of shortage of training time, continue your training as before, but cut your rest periods to the very minimum which will still allow you to meet your target times. But, in any case, try to do the very long rest, very high-quality work as often as you can, even if it means that you only have time for a few hundred yards in that particular training session.

As c.i.m. is the basis for all top-class competitive swimming, I want to close by summing up its use throughout the three main training sections of the year. The *emphasis* in each section should be as follows (but *always* use some c.i.m. of varying pace and rest times to the type you are mainly using):

> *Winter period* Introduction to c.i.m. with mainly over-the-distance work at about 80 per cent pace with fairly short rests
>
> *Pre-competitive period* Gradually work up to 90 per cent pace with longer rests
>
> *Competitive period* Very high-quality (95 per cent), with long rests

Having said that, I now want you to bear something else in the forefront of your mind—variety. Do not be a slave to the basic pattern I have given above or to the example schedules I have quoted. Do as much medley swimming and sectional work (arms-only, legs-only) as you possibly can, but make sure that you are still *working* and not just coasting up and down.

In closing, it may help you to bear in mind the following rules of training.

1. Do not miss a session unless it is absolutely necessary to do so. You are only cheating yourself, and you will remember that missed session the next time you stand on the block for a race
2. Train in a group as often as possible
3. When you are away from the pool, try to have other interests which take your mind off swimming. It is excellent to come back to the pool mentally refreshed as well as physically rested

4. Get plenty of sleep. About eight to ten hours is the minimum requirement
5. Avoid cigarettes and alcohol totally
6. Eat regular meals of the type discussed in the chapter on food

Finally I would like to quote two little sayings which I tried to remember when I was competing: 'Hard training takes the wishbone out and puts the backbone in'; and 'A quitter never wins. A winner never quits.'

6 Reaching a Peak

I believe in working for one real 'peak', and the competitive period is where we begin to sharpen up for this peak. All our training, thoughts and aims should be directed towards this event or events and the target time we have set for it. I think it is a valuable incentive to set yourself a particular time for your event which you feel sure, if attained, will realise your particular aim. Not only is it a good idea psychologically, but also practicably, because you can break this time down into individual sections, and work towards these in your interval training.

Let us take a simple example of a target swim of 400 yards' front crawl in four minutes. At the time of writing, this would be close to a British international-class effort, but for the moment we are only interested in the arithmetic of this example. Now this time represents 16×25 yards in 15 seconds, 8×50 in 30 seconds, 4×100 in 60 seconds, and 2×200 in two minutes. Throughout your months of training, these times would form the basis for your interval work, varying your rest periods according to your ability and fitness at any particular time. Your main aim should be consistently to achieve or better these times with no deterioration in your stroke, so that your pacing for your target swim becomes automatic. Naturally, all your repetitions should be done with push-offs and not dives.

Reaching a 'peak' is closely associated with what is

commonly known as 'tapering'. In simple language the 'taper' is the period in which the body is allowed to recover all its strength after months of hard work, and the mind is refreshed and directed solely towards the big swim. The amount of time given to the taper varies from about one to three weeks, but again it is something which only the swimmer himself can decide after experimenting. If you have trained very hard for some months, there is no doubt that tapering will be beneficial, so I strongly advise any swimmer who has worked conscientiously to taper for at least two weeks. If, however, on checking through your log book, you find that you have missed many training sessions and really have not done the work you should have done, then a taper of two to three days should be enough. As a general rule, sprinters, although they will not have done the volume of work of a distance swimmer, need a longer taper, because they are normally highly strung individuals, who need to be as sharp as a new pin to produce their best performances.

Now I am going to consider a three-week taper for our swimmer who is aiming at a time of four minutes for the 400 yards.

Week 3 to Week 2   A really easy week of very varied swimming, none at more than 75 per cent pace. Very little C.I.M., but any that is done should be under the distance at the target pace, but with plenty of rest. Check stroke technique and number of strokes per length at target pace.

At the end of the week a very high-quality time trial should be done over 4 × 100. The first 100 should be done with a dive in about 56 seconds. Immediately he finishes, the swimmer should walk or glide five or six yards out

83

from the wall, while the coach tells him the time and adds any other brief piece of advice. He then swims in to the wall again and the watch restarts as he turns, so that his time for each of the next three 100s includes the turn each time. Target time for each 100 is 60 seconds *maximum*, but less if possible. The aggregate swimming plus turning time should therefore come out at approximately 3 minutes 55 seconds, with only a maximum of 45 seconds' rest (3 × 15 seconds approximately) during the swim.

The following points should be noted:

1. We are in fact aiming within the target time of four minutes, because there will almost inevitably be a slight dropping-off in efficiency when the four 100s are strung together with no stops. And it is interesting to note that George Haines, American Olympic coach of Don Schollander, who won five gold medals on front crawl in 1964 and 1968, also believed in having Schollander beat the set times, when working back from the total target time.

2. This type of 'broken-swim' time trial achieves two important aims, in that it gets a near 100 per cent effort from the swimmer without his having to do a full-distance time trial, which most swimmers do not like a short time before their big event.

3. If the time by the above method is about five per cent slower than expected—or, in this case, about 4 minutes 8 seconds—then more rest is indicated, so the easy swimming should continue for another week.

Week 2 to Week 1 If the swimmer's form in the time trial has been good, the training can be slightly intensified during this week. There will still be plenty of easy, varied

84

swimming, but some 90 per cent and 95 per cent pace repetitions under the distance, with plenty of rest, can be added. Near the end of this week, another time trial should be done over 2 × 200 in the same manner as the 4 × 100 the previous week. The first 200 with a dive in about 1 minute 57 seconds, and the second with push-off in two minutes.

Last 7–8 days before race Similar training to previous week, but reduce the amount. A sprinter might concentrate on 50s and 25s at 95 per cent and 100 per cent respectively with plenty of rest, and our 400 man would do similar 100s and 50s. About three to four days before the race comes the final time trial. A 300 swim is aimed at in three minutes minus, with the usual 15 seconds or so of rest before the final turn and push-off 100 in under 60 seconds.

Continue with but decrease the fast work for the next two days and simply do an easy swim, or rest completely, on the day before the race.

The work has now been done and, if it has been properly carried out, you should now be a fit, well-rested swimmer, hungry for your big race and the achievement of your ambitions.

7 Race Day

There are many small ways in which the work done over months and even years could be destroyed by a stupid action on the day of the big race. Make sure, therefore, that you have a regular plan for this day and always try to stick to it. Now I believe that it is as damaging to have too elaborate a timetable as to have none at all. If you insist on having outlandish and unnecessary things in your pre-race programme, you will certainly find some day that for one reason or another you cannot fulfil it completely. You may not be able to have that hot bath half an hour before the race, or that shoulder massage, or you may forget your 'special' food preparation, which is impossible to replace. When you cannot follow your programme exactly, you begin to worry, and your whole race attitude then becomes wrong, which is the worst fault of all.

Having explained that, now let me stress that your race preparations should be simple, logical and flexible enough for you to be able to follow them almost exactly, no matter which pool, town or country you are competing in. If you follow the following basic rules, you should not go far wrong.

Mental preparation
This is the most important single factor in any kind of human endeavour, whether it be swimming a certain

distance in a certain time, doing well in business, or playing a musical instrument well. *Everything* depends on whether you want something badly enough. Superbly fit, well-trained athletes are often defeated in competition by less well-prepared and less talented performers simply because the latter have that extra something in their psychological make-up which drives them to victory.

Although some people have the right attitude in their natural character I am convinced that it can be taught, but you yourself must be the teacher. Train yourself to think *positively*. By that I mean that you *must* have the confidence to decide what you are going to do in training, and more importantly in a race, and then to do it. Do not think in terms of what you *might* do, or what your excuses could be if you do not accomplish what you set out to do.

Of course you will meet opponents whom you know have always been much better than you in the past, but this must not affect your own positive thinking, which must drive you to obtain 100 per cent effort from your body, and the best performance of which you are capable. You must leave the pool after the race thinking, 'Well, that is the best that I can do at the moment', regardless of where you finished. The 'at the moment' is important, because you should always be looking ahead to further training and improvement.

You will not go far wrong if you always bear in mind that if a race is worth swimming in at all, then it is worth your maximum efforts. If, however, you have heats and finals in one session and you are certain of qualifying without a 100 per cent effort, then obviously in this case it is permissible to save yourself for the final.

The following two little anecdotes from my own experience as a commentator and journalist should show you very clearly the importance of mental approach.

A few years ago a team of swimmers from the United States came to an invitation meeting in Britain. They were all performers of the highest class and one in particular could have won his race without unduly exerting himself, as he was very much faster than any of his opponents. One journalist asked him, 'Do you intend to do your best or just swim to win?' The 17-year-old American looked genuinely surprised and a little upset by the question. 'Whether I'm first or last, Sir, you can always be sure that I've done my very best.' He won easily, and narrowly missed the world record.

The second story concerns our own Martyn Woodroffe *(38)*, who went to the Mexico Olympics having apparently no chance of a medal. But he had always been a 100 per cent trier, and in spite of swimming disappointingly in three early races in Mexico, he still approached the 200 metres butterfly final with an unshaken determination to do his best-ever swim. His determination brought him a silver medal, and he was only a few inches from the gold.

If you can combine this attitude with hard training, then your success is assured. On race day, most of all, you should consciously think as positively as the two swimmers in my anecdotes. It may help put you in the right frame of mind to read about great sportsmen in the past, so take a book on that subject with you to the meeting, and remember, they just had one head, two arms and two legs, the same as you!

Rest

Take at least as much sleep as you normally have, and don't be afraid to have an extra hour or so in bed after you wake, if you feel like it. Take additional rest through-

38 Martyn Woodroffe (Cardiff) pictured in Mexico City just after winning his silver medal in the 200 metres butterfly

out the day, and try to cultivate an interest in reading—as well as being physically resting, it is also a good way of taking your mind off the tension of the race. Do *not* go sightseeing, as this is an excellent way of unwittingly tiring yourself.

Food

If we assume that your event is in the evening, then your normal breakfast and lunch can be taken, but whenever your race may be, it is advisable to have your last meal not less than three hours before, and for reasons which I explain in my chapter on food it is also beneficial to eat certain things in this last meal.

Swimming

I favour two swims on race day, the first in the morning after breakfast, and the second—the warm-up—about 30–45 minutes before the event.

The first swim should, if possible, be in the race pool, particularly if it is not familiar to you. Obviously it will not be a hard training session, but what is done is really up to the swimmer and how much he feels like doing, with the emphasis being on too little rather than too much. About 800–1000 yards of mixed swimming is a fairly typical amount. Try to swim in the same lane as in your race, and practise starts and turns. Note any pool markings which may help you during the race.

The warm-up is an absolutely essential part of any preparation for maximum effort. Not 'tapering' properly and not warming-up properly were, I am now certain, the two major mistakes I made in my own career, and the improvement in my performances when I did employ these aids was quite striking.

Most swimmers are naturally a little wary of doing anything tiring in the period immediately (say one hour) before a race. But do remember this: you are, or should be, a superbly fit, well-trained athlete by the time you reach your big event. You are accustomed to a great deal of interval training and your body should recover *completely* in a very short time after a light, but very high-quality session of work. And that is what your warm-up should consist of. The following might be used by a sprinter:

a. 400–500 arms, legs and full stroke (i.e., a *total* of 400–500 yards)
b. 3 × 50 (plenty of rest, at 80 per cent, 90 per cent and 95 per cent pace)
c. 100 very easy
d. 4 × 25 (95 per cent, 95 per cent, 100 per cent, 100 per cent)

After the swim, dry thoroughly, relax, and try to keep the body temperature high, right up to the time you hit the water in your event.

Shaving
It has become increasingly popular in recent years to shave the hair off the arms and legs (and chest, in men) in order to cut down water resistance. I never did it, and originally I believed that it was mainly a psychological fad. More recently, however, scientific tests do seem to indicate that there is a real speed benefit to be derived from this. Some coaches put the improvement as high as one to two seconds over 100 metres, although my own feeling is that this is probably an exaggeration. However, I do advocate the use of this technique, and recommend

that it should be done on the morning of your race, before you have been in the water on that day. There is no doubt that it provides a great psychological boost, and the feeling in the water is also quite striking.

Sportsmanship

Not everyone can be a winner, and although you will be doing your utmost to be first home every time, when you do not make it you must accept defeat gracefully. The disappointment of seeing your hopes dashed can be overwhelming, but your bedroom is the only place to be overwhelmed if you really feel badly. At the pool you must take it like a man and give due credit to the better swimmer on that day.

On the other hand, however, you may turn out to be someone who wins most of the time, and in this situation it can be just as easy to be a bad sport by being arrogant and conceited. You may have trained very hard and have thoroughly deserved your victory, but you must not forget that some of the others may have trained even harder. The difference between a winner and a loser can be very small, and victory or defeat can be decided by apparently insignificant factors which have nothing to do with how hard you have trained. I am thinking of things like natural ability, natural shape, flotability, etc., and although I do not wish to dwell on these points, we should always remember, when things are going well for us, that somewhere along the way we probably had a little bit of luck which could have meant the difference between success and failure. Be thankful, not arrogant.

8   Food

Nowadays, when you pull up at a garage for petrol, you can choose between a large selection of petrols and oils for the car. The petrols have octane numbers (95, 97, 99, etc.) and the oils also have varying mixtures. Each engine has been built to receive one particular octane rating, and the makers tell us which is best for the car. Now the engine will run on *any* of the petrols or oils on sale at the garage, but it will be most *efficient* only on the fuel recommended by the engine manufacturer.

Our bodies are the most important engines that we will ever have to deal with, yet too often we do not obey the simple rules about the food (our fuel) that we should use.

There is no need to become a food 'faddist', who cannot eat out because he needs special foods, and who is difficult to have as a guest in one's home. The guiding principle is to eat a wide variety of foods which are as near their natural condition as possible. There are too many synthetic foods on the market in this modern age, and very often the natural goodness of the ingredients has been refined out in the manufacturing process, so whenever possible stick to natural products.

Our diet requirements fall into five main categories:

1. Protein foods, which help build body tissues, and of which the most common are meat, eggs, fish and cheese

2. Carbohydrates, which are the main source of readily available energy and are found in bread, sugar, cakes, biscuits and many fruits and vegetables

3. Fats such as butter and margarine, which help keep the body supple, and are a secondary source of energy

4. Vitamins, which control the use the body makes of its food, and which are found in fresh fruit, leafy vegetables, whole-grain cereals, butter, milk and eggs

5. Minerals which occur in small amounts in most of the above foods

A diet selected from the above would guarantee a sufficient supply of everything which is essential for our physical well-being, and so, having explained the general structure of foods, the following points should be borne in mind by the swimmer in training:

1. Proteins should be eaten daily in as large amounts as can comfortably be consumed. Many protein foods, however, are difficult to digest, so take care not to eat too much soon before swimming.

2. Although carbohydrates are the main source of readily available energy, one must not load up with them, as they are also the main depositors of fat in the body. A fairly moderate intake will normally provide enough energy even for the athlete in training, the only exception being the pre-race meal, which I will discuss later.

Two carbohydrates to be avoided in particular are white sugar and white flour and anything made with them. Substitute wholemeal flour, and get your sweetness from honey, brown sugar, raisins, figs, dates and also dried fruits. Chocolate and other confections, soft drinks or squashes should also be taken in moderation. Milk and natural fruit juices are the best pure liquid foods.

Now if you read the above once again, you will realise that the recommended foods are all readily available and you would not in any way seem a 'crank' by sticking to them, so do so and you can be sure that your 'engine' is primed to run as it was meant to.

Some coaches advise their swimmers to eat additional vitamins, but there is certainly no general scientific agreement about the benefits of this. In the case of Vitamin E, however, there is apparently strong evidence that regular dosage can increase physical efficiency, particularly with regard to endurance. For this reason I recommend a daily intake of Vitamin E, or wheatgerm oil, which has a high content of this vitamin. According to Forbes Carlisle, the well-known coach from Australia, where the use of wheatgerm oil for swimmers was pioneered, the dosage of Vitamin E should not be less than 600 milligrams per day. Wheatgerm also contains some of the Vitamin B group, which help the body to convert carbohydrate into energy.

The pre-competition meal
The pre-race meal should fulfil four main objectives:

1. It should be easily digestible
2. It should provide an additional supply of readily available energy
3. It should be easy to obtain wherever you may be called on to compete
4. It should be reasonably palatable

Bearing all these factors in mind, a semi-liquid meal consisting mainly of carbohydrates in commonly available products appears to fit the bill. My pre-race meal, therefore, taken not less than three hours before a race, would be along the following lines:

1. Porridge with plenty of sugar and/or stewed fruit
2. Two/three slices of bread/toast and jam
3. Sweet, weak coffee made almost entirely with milk

During a swimming gala many competitors suck sweets or glucose, but a recent article by the American Medical Association's Committee on Sports points out that such things draw fluid into the stomach to allow digestion. This fluid comes from the rest of the body, therefore reducing its proper balance of fluid. The committee feel strongly enough about this to recommend the avoidance of eating *anything* during a meeting. If you feel nervous, they suggest sweet tea with lemon, or not more than half a glass of water at any time if you are thirsty.

9   Starts and Turns

All competitive swimming races begin with a start, usually a dive from a raised block, and all have at least one turn during their course. It is surely clear, therefore, that these two aspects of swimming competition *must* be up to standard, or you are at a serious disadvantage before the race even begins.

Starting has always been done reasonably well on all strokes by most swimmers, but for many years turning, particularly on front crawl, was a sadly neglected part of most swimmers' preparation for competition. Nowadays, however, most coaches are very conscious of the importance of this aspect of swimming, and because of the resulting improvement, it is essential that no swimmer should be found wanting in these skills, or he will be carrying a handicap which will undoubtedly cost him races throughout his competitive career.

THE START—*procedure*

There are only two commands in any normal start, namely 'Take your marks' and 'Go' (or pistol shot, whistle or klaxon). On the first command you should *immediately* take up your *final* starting position and await the second command. Usually you will be starting from a raised block (except backstroke), and there is nothing in the rules to prevent you from standing on it, even with your feet in their final position, *before* the 'Take your marks'.

Some starters, however, insist that you either stand behind the block, till they give the first command, or, if they permit you to stand on the block, you must stand back from the edge, so that you have to step forward at 'Take your marks'.

It is easy to discover in advance, either by observation or enquiry, which method the starter favours, and although, as I have pointed out, there is nothing in the rules to prevent you from standing directly on the block before any command has been given, you must remember that at that point the starter is in charge and you must follow his wishes. Obviously, therefore, you must be quite happy to accept any of the above procedures for starting, so practise them all in your training programme.

If there is a false start, you will be recalled by one of the four starting signals, and a rope will also be dropped across the course about 10 yards from the start. Return to the start immediately, or step down if you did not enter the water, and await the starter's further instructions. On the third and subsequent false starts, anyone who enters the water is disqualified, regardless of whether he was an offender in the previous starts.

I have always considered swimmers who regularly cause false starts, at best poorly prepared in their starting techniques, and at worst potential cheats who are trying to gain an unfair advantage, so make sure you are in neither category.

All the above procedure refers also to backstroke, although the start is always from a position in the water facing the starting end of the pool.

Stance ('Take your marks')

The feet should be about six inches apart, with most of the toes gripping the edge of the block *(39)*. When standing relaxed, most people have the feet pointing slightly outwards, but in this position only the big toes would be able to grip a starting block, so it will be necessary to have your feet absolutely parallel for the correct stance. When you are properly positioned there should be a feeling of real solidity, and when practising, you should be able to rock the body fairly vigorously in any direction without overbalancing. Slight bending at the knees will increase your ability to balance.

The body is usually bent into approximately a right

39 It is important that both feet should have a firm grip of the starting block. Note that the feet are parallel, and at least three toes are gripping the edge very tightly

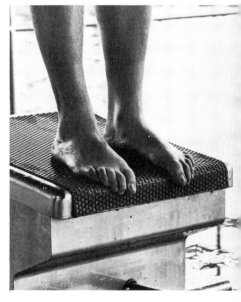

angle at the waist, the arms either hang straight down from the shoulders or back alongside the trunk, and the eyes look at the target entry point in the water *(40)*.

Only in the arm position is there any real difference of opinion among swimmers and coaches, and much though I have interested myself in this subject over more than 20 years in swimming, I have never been convinced that there is any real advantage one way or another. I think nowadays it is slightly more popular to have the arms in the forward position, so we will take that as the recommended stance.

The heels must be down, but the weight should be mainly on the balls of the feet.

The dive (41–45)
On the 'Go' the main points to bear in mind are as follows:

1. Get as far out in the dive as possible and it will help to keep the head up at this stage to maintain height.
2. Stretch the whole body from fingertips to toes. I always tell my pupils to imagine they are forming a spear.
3. Drop the head between the arms immediately before they enter the water.

40 (top left)   The position I favoured at 'Take your marks', although it is perhaps more popular nowadays to carry the arms in front of the body.   41 (top right)   On the 'Go' the arms are flung back and the body begins to fall forward. If the arms are held in front of the body, it is usual for them to make a circular motion all in front of the body *before the fling forward.   42 (below)   The arms are very forcefully thrown forward, and the main drive comes from the legs when the body is approaching a position parallel to the water*

43 (above) Notice the height a correct leg drive can give. The body is stretched to the maximum, but the head is still above the level of the arms. *44 (below)* As the body begins to fall, the head is dropped down between the arms immediately before the shallow dive

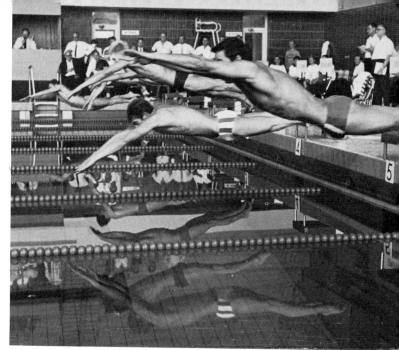

45 Note the different techniques at the start of this 100 metres freestyle in the annual European Six Nations match in Germany. If the picture is turned upside down, Bobby McGregor can be seen in reflection with his feet still on Block 3. He won in spite of this slowish start

4. Make the entry shallow enough so that the forward momentum will continue after the whole body is immersed.

Common faults

The commonest fault in beginners is to believe that the racing dive is, in fact, not a head-first entry into the water, but a belly-first entry! This type of 'belly flop' not only leads to sore tummies, but is also quite inefficient, because if you land flat on the water, you will have no forward momentum at all, and will therefore have to start swimming almost from a dead stop. This type of dive is caused by using the leg power from the block and the arm fling, to drive the body immediately upwards, when in fact one must wait until the body has fallen forward with the lower legs almost parallel with the water surface before applying the leg push.

The causes of the arched 'jack-knife' dive are exactly the same as the 'belly flop', only in the former case the diver at the last moment lifts the hips to prevent a hurtful entry.

Another common fault is having the arms apart on entry. Clearly this impedes proper streamlining, however slightly, and should be avoided. To ensure that the arms were really together, I always locked my right thumb between the thumb and first finger of the left hand, and pulled hard to stretch the arms forward.

The pick-up

The speed on entry of a good dive is obviously very much faster than anyone can swim, so do not begin to swim immediately you hit the water. Some beginners even have the legs thrashing *before* they hit the water, and this, of course, can only hinder your streamlining and slow you down.

The exact point at which the stroke 'picks-up' the momentum of the dive really cannot be taught—it must be decided by the swimmer himself by experience and 'feel'—but there are two points to be borne in mind for all the strokes except the breast stroke: firstly, the legs should begin just before the arms; secondly, the body must be

46　The push-off and starting dive position on breast stroke immediately after the arm pull. Note that the arms have taken a much longer pull than when on the surface, and will in fact come right to the thighs. ▪There has been no kick so far

47　The legs and arms have recovered together, and now the arms are stretching forward as the legs begin their drive backwards. The body must reach the surface on the impetus of this kick, for any further arm or leg movement while the body is still submerged would result in disqualification

completely on the surface as the first arm action begins. If you find that you are still under water as you pull, then the dive was not shallow enough.

The breast stroke is different from the other strokes insofar as there is a definite advantage in doing a full stroke (i.e., one arm pull and one leg kick) under water. The advantage lies in being able to do a much longer arm pull than is done on the surface. As the dive momentum slows down, the arms begin their pull from the arms-stretched-forward position right back to the thighs. As the arms recover, the legs give their normal kick, which *must* bring the swimmer to the surface, for even a part of a second stroke under water causes disqualification on breast stroke only *(46, 47)*.

Backstroke

Much of the above also refers to the backstroke start *(48–53)*, in spite of the obvious difference in starting position. The feet are usually placed one above the other about six inches apart, with the ball of the lower foot overlapping the heel of the higher foot. Both feet *must* be under the surface, or the starter will ask you to adjust your position. The hand should grasp the rail or scum channel firmly at about shoulder width, or the starting handles which are usually provided at the front of modern starting blocks.

On the 'Take your marks' you should pull up into a tense ball with the chin on the knees. This position must be practised a great deal to ensure that your feet will not slip when the big drive from the wall comes.

On the 'Go' push *up* and *out*, with the arms flung and stretched straight back and the head between the arms. You must ensure that there is still forward momentum

48 (left)   The relaxed position of the backstroke start, while waiting for the 'Take your marks'.   49 (right)   On the first word of command, the body is curled up like a spring and pulled nearer the wall. Note that one foot is slightly higher than the other, for greater security when the big push comes

as the arms hit the water, otherwise you will have done the equivalent of a 'belly flop', and for the same reasons.

Two final points on starts. No good starter will give the 'Go' till all the competitors are perfectly still, so don't be the one who holds up the whole line by fidgeting. And finally, I advise you to practise high jumps on the spot with toes pointed and legs straight, to get the feel of

50 (above) On the 'Go', the 'spring' is released. As the arms are flung backwards, the aim is to gain height, then distance. 51 (below) As the arms come together, the head goes right back and the dive flattens out

52, 53 Backstroke starts: above, Clive Rushton (Rochdale) in action against West Germany; below, Sylvia Platt (Hyde), nearest the camera, and Janet Franklin (Taunton)

54 Both hands have simultaneously grabbed the channel, and already the body is turning on its side to allow the right shoulder to lead into the push-off. When there is no channel, the palms of the hands are placed flat on the wall, but the impetus of the stroke must be allowed to drive the body close to the wall before the turn is begun, to ensure a good push-off

really thrusting with the legs. Too many swimmers do not use all their available leg power on the start. The drive required is every bit as vigorous as that needed to push the body straight upwards, and I always found jumps on the spot a valuable way of putting the right idea across to my pupils.

THE TURN

Just a few years ago any discussion about turns in competitive swimming would certainly have been both lengthy and full of disagreement. Recently, however,

55   The body is now fully on the side, and the feet firmly planted on the wall. Note the upward position of the face giving completely unrestricted inhalation. Remember that the body must be flat again before the feet leave the wall

there has been fairly widespread agreement as to what are the best methods of turning, even in front-crawl swimming, where formerly about half a dozen turns were in common use.

Breast stroke and butterfly

The turns for these strokes *(54, 55)* are extremely similar, mainly because the rules call for a similar touch by both hands with the body flat on the surface before the turn commences.

The movements of the turn itself are quite logical. As

both hands touch, allow the elbows to bend so that the body as it turns comes close into the wall and the feet begin to place themselves flat on the wall behind the buttocks. If there is a rail or scum channel, you can pull yourself in and therefore turn faster, but remember that many pools, and certainly international-class ones, have a flat wall, so you must be proficient at turning without using these fixtures.

It is permissible to leave the 'flat-on-the-breast' position, as the time between hand touch and feet leaving the wall during the turn is exempt from the law, and most swimmers therefore do not complete the body turn on the wall. They push off with one shoulder leading, partly on their sides, but are flat on the breast again just before the feet leave the wall. Disqualification would result, of course, if the body were still on the side after the push-off.

At this point the butterfly and breast-stroke techniques differ, for the latter will have a complete stroke under water (as at the start), but on the butterfly it is better to surface as the push-off begins to lose momentum. Naturally, the breast stroke push-off will be slightly deeper than the butterfly one, to allow the single under-water stroke.

A forward somersault turn is sometimes used on both these strokes, with a half twist on the second half of the somersault, to bring the body back on the breast before the feet leave the side. It has never really become popular, however, and I think this is mainly because there is an ever-present risk of disqualification and also because it is particularly difficult and exhausting to perform with both arms in front of the body throughout the movement. With the alternate arm action of the backstroke and front crawl, however, while the forward arm is leading into the somersault, the other arm is alongside the body balancing it and pulling it through the turn, and this makes similar turns on these two strokes easier and more reliable.

Backstroke
Backstrokers have always been the fastest and most reliable of all swimmers in executing their turns. I am sure that this is simply because they *have* to be efficient, or the result could quite easily be broken fingers or cracked skulls. Self-preservation is clearly a greater incentive than mere will to win!

There are two backstroke turns which are acknowledged to be very fast, but one has such a high danger of disqualification that it is virtually not used at all. The turn which is in almost universal use is usually called the 'back flip', and consists of a half back somersault followed by a half twist *(56–58)*.

As the backstroker approaches the wall he will pass under the warning flags about five yards out, and this gives an exact indication of his position. I definitely recommend, however, that in addition to placing yourself according to the flags, you should also have *one* look over your shoulder to make certain of *exactly* how far you are from the wall, and, more important, which hand will make contact first. The one glance should naturally be taken after the feet have passed the flags, for by this time it will be easy to estimate the contact arm correctly.

The hand should aim to touch the wall about a foot below the surface, and the head and shoulders follow it into the beginning of a back somersault. When the head and shoulders are completely submerged, the body pivots on them, the legs are lifted over the surface, and the feet are slapped on the wall at about the same point as the hand originally touched. The arms are now both stretched out behind, with the head between them, and the push-off drives the spear-shaped body from the wall.

56　*The first stage of the backstroke turn, showing the head well back, the body arched, and the legs being drawn clear of the water*

Normally, swimmers who touch with the right hand put the head and shoulders back slightly to the right, and the legs will therefore come over slightly to the left. With

57 As the feet are being flung over, the touching arm is still in contact with the wall, giving stability and leverage to the turn, and the pull of the right arm is holding the body close to the wall and assisting the speed of the spin

a left-hand touch, the movements are, of course, reversed. Some swimmers even put the right touching hand down behind the left shoulder, and the legs therefore come over slightly to the right. I mention these points not to confuse the reader, but to show that provided one follows the basic movements described in the previous paragraph, there will be virtually no effect on the speed of the turn, Whether you put the head and shoulders back to one side

58   *As the feet pass the central position, both arms quickly move behind the head and prepare for a spear-like push-off*

or the other, or even dead centre, should be governed to a great extent by how comfortable you feel in executing the turn.

Probably the fastest turn of all is the back-crawl tumble turn. As the swimmer approaches the wall, and has decided he is going to touch with the right hand, just before contact he turns the body on to his left side and swings the right arm across to touch below the left shoulder. *After* the hand touch, he completes the full twist of the body on to his breast and then does a complete forward somersault before pushing off quite normally on his back.

A recent clarification of the rules permits the body before the turn (i.e., the hand touch) to go fully on to the side, but not beyond a 90-degree angle with the surface. It is obviously very difficult, when swinging the arm across the chest, to prevent the body from going past the perpendicular before the touch, and it is this which has given this turn a higher rate of disqualification than any other, on any stroke.

With the rules as they are at present, I must advise against the use of this turn in competition, although I would be in favour of practising it during training, simply because executing skills of this type is an excellent way of developing general 'watermanship' and in this case would help to increase confidence in body control in any turn.

Front crawl
The front crawl has seen a greater variety of turns than all the other three strokes put together. In the early fifties, however, the 'tumble' turn *(59–61)* was introduced in America for sprint races, and gradually its use was

117

extended to middle-distance events. Since about 1964 it has been used almost universally by men and women for all distances. The advent of this turn has been the greatest single cause of the improvement in front-crawl turning in recent years. It is so much faster than any of its predecessors that swimmers now realise that they must tumble well to stay in the race.

59　Note how the head has gone right forward and downwards in this tumble turn. Both hands have been pulling to increase the speed of spin of the somersault, and in completing their pull, they momentarily break surface

Another helpful factor in recent years has been the ruling that it is no longer necessary to touch with the *hand* in turning. 'Any part of the body' is now the official wording for front crawl, and naturally this means the feet for the fast turner.

The tumble consists of a forward somersault straight in to the wall with a half twist during the final part of the

60 Note how the legs appear absolutely in unison, and fairly straight

somersault and the beginning of the push-off, to bring the body back on the breast. It is not an easy turn to do well, and the young swimmer must persevere with his practice in order to become fully proficient.

In learning any very fast movement (e.g., a golf swing), it is better to concentrate on a few main points and then to allow constant practice to iron out any imperfections. It is very easy to confuse your brain by trying to think of too many things at one time, and the result is nearly always disaster. With the tumble, the basic movements to concentrate on are as follows:

1. When the leading hand is about one foot from the wall, thrust the head down under that armpit and at the same time lift the hips

2. Keep the legs fairly straight and fling the feet at the wall as your body is beginning to turn on to its side during the last part of the somersault

3. Bring the hands together and push off with the feet in the same position at which they hit the wall

If you are a sprinter, it is essential to be able to turn with either hand leading, so practise with both. In middle and distance swimming, however, it is quite easy slightly to adjust the stroke, so as to reach the wall always on the same hand.

Only experience will teach you how far from the wall to commence the turn, but you must be close enough to ensure a good bend at the knees for the push-off.

If you experience a need for breath when turning on the non-breathing arm, it will hinder you little to snatch another breath before you go into the wall. This is much better than being in distress on the push-off and having to surface early.

The whole action should be smooth and continuous, and if you think of yourself as a rubber ball hitting a wall then you will have the right idea.

61   The feet are thrown very forcefully against the wall. Here the left foot is slightly leading the right as the body begins to turn on its left side for the push-off

10　Diving

Swimming and diving are as inseparable as Jack and Jill, but only because both sports need a swimming pool and its equipment for the best presentation of competitions. The activities themselves are otherwise quite different, and this is why few swimmers become competent *competitive* divers and vice-versa.

All important aquatic meetings, however, include both sports, because they are governed by the same national and international organisations, and therefore swimmers are constantly meeting and mixing with the diving fraternity. Now competitive swimming is very easy to understand, because anybody can see who has won a race, but diving is very much more complicated, and I think swimmers should make the effort to understand this wonderful sport.

The main aim of this chapter will therefore be to set down the rules, regulations and procedure of competitive diving, but I hope also that some readers may be induced to take up the sport seriously.

Position of dives

Dives can be performed either straight, piked, tucked, or, in the case of twist dives, in an unspecified position.

The straight position need not be absolutely straight, as it is permissible to hollow the back slightly in certain dives, but under no circumstances can there be any bending at the hips or knees.

In the piked position the body must bend at the hips, but the knees must again be straight. The arm position is left to the diver, and most either hold them out to the side or clasp the hands behind the knees.

The tucked position demands bending at the hips and knees, so that the body forms a kind of ball, with the hands clasping the shins. The knees should be together, but some divers in the highest class still open them slightly in order to be able to spin faster, in spite of the fact that the judges should deduct one to two points if they notice it.

Many dives may also be performed in the 'flying' position, which means that, immediately the flight begins, the diver holds a position with the arms stretched sideways (commonly known as the 'swallow' position), before continuing with the dive in any of the three previously explained positions.

Groups of dives

There are six groups of dives, and the diving regulations are so devised that in competition the divers are tested on all the relevant groups:

Forward Group (1)   All dives with forward rotation from a forward take-off

Backward Group (2)   All dives with backward rotation from a backward take-off

Reverse Group (3)   All dives with backward rotation from a forward take-off

Inward Group (4)   All dives with forward rotation from a backward take-off

These are obviously the only four ways in which a dive can be originated from the board, but if the dive includes a twist, then regardless of other factors, it goes into the Twist Group (5).

The final category is the Armstand Group (6) which is used only from the firmboard.

Degree of difficulty

If one diver performs a plain dive very well, and another does a $3\frac{1}{2}$ somersault equally well, then obviously the second diver should benefit from having done a much more difficult movement. This is done by giving each dive a degree of difficulty—sometimes called the tariff—according to how difficult it is in relation to the other dives in the tables. The tariffs range from 1·3 to 2·9, and the diver's score is multiplied by this figure. It is important to note, however, that the judges make no allowance for tariff, but merely score the dive on its performance. The Chief Recorder calculates the score including the tariff.

Dives and their numbers

Every dive in the Springboard and Highboard Tables is identified by a number, and this is usually shown on scoreboards to avoid the use of long phrases such as 'An inward $1\frac{1}{2}$ somersault, with 2 twists'. Most dives have a three-figure number—e.g., 213—but all twist dives have four—e.g., 5231.

With three-figure numbers, except armstand dives, the first digit indicates the group, the second whether 'flying' (1) or non-flying (0), and the third the number of half somersaults. Our first example, therefore, is a flying backward $1\frac{1}{2}$ somersaults.

With twist dives the first number is always 5, indicating

the twist group, the second gives its sub-grouping according to the four main groups, the third the number of *half* somersaults and the fourth the number of *half* twists. The second example is therefore a backward $1\frac{1}{2}$ somersaults with half twist.

The armstand group is slightly different from the other three-figure categories, because like the twist group, there are no 'flying' dives, so there is no need for a number for this position. A typical example would be dive 632, where the 6 tells us that it is an armstand, the 3 that it is a reverse group dive, and the 2 that it includes one complete somersault. It is therefore an armstand, cut-through and reverse dive.

If one adds the position of the dive and the tariff, a typical appearance on the scoreboard might be 413 c 2·0, meaning an inward flying $1\frac{1}{2}$ somersaults in the tuck position, with a degree of difficulty of 2·0. Remember that the letter D, used only in twisting dives, means that the diver may select any position for the performance of the dive.

Judging
For all major competitions there must be seven judges, who are under the direct control of the referee. When a dive has been completed, he gives a blast on a whistle to indicate that all the judges must show their markings immediately.

The chief recorder copies each score into the competitor's sheet, strikes out the highest and lowest score, then using a mathematical ready reckoner, he finds the average of the remaining five scores and multiplies it by the tariff of the dive. For example, with scores of $5\frac{1}{2}$, 7, 7, 8, 6, 7, 8, the $5\frac{1}{2}$ and one of the 8s are eliminated, leaving a total of 35 points from five judges. The average is therefore 35 divided by five, giving 7, which is then multiplied by the tariff. If the tariff were 2·5, the total for the dive would be 17·5.

Competition procedure

Springboard diving   In all major springboard competitions, both men and women must perform 10 dives, five of which are compulsory and five voluntary. The five required dives are always: 1. forward dive; 2. back dive; 3. reverse dive; 4. inward dive; 5. forward dive with half twist, and they may be performed either straight (a), piked (b) or tucked (c). The voluntary dives are chosen by the diver himself, and he will naturally try to achieve as high a tariff total as possible, within the limits of his ability.

Highboard diving   Men must perform six voluntaries, one from each group, with a tariff total of not more than 11·2, and a further four voluntaries, each from a different group, with no tariff limit.

In the women's competition there are four required dives: 1. forward dive; 2. back dive; 3. reverse dive; 4. inward dive, all of which may be done in any position. These are followed by three voluntary dives, each from a different group, with no tariff limit.

Basic or key dives

There are six dives which have been selected by the Amateur Swimming Association as being essential to rapid and sound development in diving, and they are as follows:

1. Forward dive piked
2. Back dive piked
3. Reverse dive piked
4. Inward dive piked
5. Forward dive, one twist straight
6. Armstand somersault tucked
7. Armstand cut-through tucked

Any young diver must aim to become completely proficient at these dives before moving on to the high-tariff movements, which nowadays are essential if you want to enter a high class of competition.

At the beginning of this book I stressed the importance of having a coach to watch over your swimming development, and I think this is as good a point as any to make in my closing comments on diving. Although it might just be possible to become a really good swimmer by reading some books and then training hard, I think it would be impossible to do this in diving, because it is essential for someone to *see* what you are doing.

Conclusion

When I was asked to embark on this book by the publisher, my first reaction was that it would mean too much work, and I was too busy anyway. Then I began to think of how much swimming has given me, and I quickly realised that here was a challenge that I could not ignore, for it offered me the opportunity of helping some aspiring young swimmers perhaps to experience the many benefits which swimming brought me.

I hope what I have written will encourage you to accept the challenges which this great sport offers you. The cornerstones of your hopes should be self-discipline and determination and, believe me, these factors can more than make up for not having webbed feet!

I hope you enjoyed reading the book and I hope you have learned something from my experience (and my mistakes!). May I leave you with this thought—a performance which seems impossible today, will be commonplace in a few years time, so why wait? It's up to you.